What did you say my name was?
(The True Story of Life after Amnesia)

What did you say your name was?
(The True Story of Life after Amnesia)

Shawna Lynn Stewart

This book was printed in the United States of America.

Softcover ISBN   978-0-9831791-7-7

To order additional copies of this book, contact:
New View Publishing
www.newviewpublishing.net
Info@newviewpublishing.net

For my family. Your love gives me the strength that I need. You patience gave the freedom to find out who I was.

Thanks to Kathy Zygo for the beautiful picture on the front cover. I love you.

Dedication

I would like to dedicate this book to my Family and Friends. Without your support I would have remained lost.

Preface

On March 24th 1995 Shawna died.

On March 25th 1995 Shawna was brought back to life.

They say Death is peaceful but what happens when Death is only for an instant? What becomes of that person when they are no longer the person they once were?

Shawna Stewart shares with her readers her life story that at times seems all too unreal. But for her it was reality, a reality that continues to haunt her.

An autobiography by Shawna Stewart

Chapter 1

As a young Mother Shawna was forced into a life that would leave her uncertain. Her life changed when she became victim to horrible disease, "Eclampsia". Shawna died that night only to be reborn someone she didn't know. Because of the severity of her complications of the disease; she lost her memory. After 7 seven years of going to different doctors she finally was told that she would never regain the memory that she lost. She found herself living in a world she didn't know, with people she didn't know.

At first she let the memory loss controlled her and she did not tell her family what was happening. After a few years she finally admitted to her family what was happening and to her surprise they were very supportive and tried to help her remember as much they could.

For years her biggest supporter was her Mother. Her mother would take out pictures and tell wonderful stories to her; anything that she thought would spark a memory. The memories never came. But, Shawna still liked hearing the stories and often called her Mother to hear more. Unfortunately, her Mother died soon after, leaving Shawna more heartbroken then ever. Not only had she lost her Mother once, she had now lost her forever. Within months she lost her Uncle, sister and brother, all of which she had become close too. Shawna now would have to fight a whole knew disease; depression.

It took over a year before Shawna would speak of any past memories because she felt as it to be useless, as to her once she finally was getting to know someone they would pass away. Shawna's husband was determined to get her back on the right track, so he did everything in his power to get her out of her depression and back on track with her life. After a while Shawna realized that he was right and decided the best thing for her was to live with what was in front of her and let the others continue on with her mom's mission to teach her the past. Her family never gave up, they tired and tried to help her remember, but the memories remained lost inside her.

It wasn't until years after the whole horrible ordeal started that Shawna finally gave into the inevitable and gave in; deciding to leave her past behind her and make new memories. The battle was hard at first as she continued to look at old photographs of her older boys and realized that she would never have the memory of their childhood again.

After years of disbelieve that this could happen to her, she finally decided to do something about it. She returned to school and with the suggestion from her son she began writing again. She now lives the life of someone whom is new to everyone. That of a stranger.

This is her story:

WHAT DID YOU SAY MY NAME WAS?

Chapter 2

There are very few things I remember about my life and the ones I do remember I wish I could forget. Sometimes when I think back to the memories that remain, I wonder how many others are lost, and then think how lucky I am that they are. My memories jump from year to year, leaving me empty from most.

My story begins here, because it is the first memory I have. I do not remember being any younger then eleven or twelve years of age.

I have been told stories and have seen pictures. But nothing seems to help. One of the pictures I adore. It is a picture of my sister and me standing in front of what looks to be an old shed. It turns out

that it was our house when we were five
and six years old. Neither one of us was
wearing shoes, but we had on two
beautiful little dresses that my mother
had made us. The picture reminds me of
a place way back in the woods
somewhere. If I remember right I think I
was told we lived in Texas somewhere.
What I love about the picture is that by
looking at it you can see we were poor,
but my sister and I looked happy.

My story begins in Las Vegas
somewhere around 1979; the year I am
uncertain of. My family lives in Las
Vegas, but I can not tell you how long
we have been living here. Both of my
parents are bricklayers and work almost
everyday. My Father is an alcoholic and
drinks everyday, all day; in fact he
usually continues to drink until he passes
out for the night. Sometimes it is a good
day and no one gets screamed at and my
Mother and Father do not fight, other
nights, I wish I could run away.

My sister and I share a room that
is just outside the living room. Once you
pass the living room you must pass

through our room to get to the kitchen, the bathroom or any other part of the house. We have no privacy. There is no door to separate us from the other parts of the house, so I had always hated that room. It is not really because of the lack of privacy, but something about the room or possibly it is the house that gives me the creeps

I am a very quiet girl and usually like to play by myself. My favorite thing to do is to act like I am a gymnast. For hours I would play outside on a make-shift beam doing cartwheels, and anything else that I had taught myself to do.

It is five o'clock in the afternoon and my parents are home early. My Dad is drunk as usual; his choice of poison is Coors. Something about him is different today and I have feeling that I need to stay away from him. For hours I play outside, but once the sun sets I know I must go inside. We only live a mile from the downtown strip and it is not safe for a child as young as I to play outside without a companion. I dread going in so

I sit on the porch as long as I can before I am told that I must come in and get ready for school tomorrow.

I quickly walk past my dad who is sitting in the living room drinking another beer and watching TV. He looks up at me and with a smile, he asks where I have been all day. The smell of alcohol instantly fills the air and sickens my stomach. I ignore his question and continue to my bedroom. He is drunk, so I know in a minute he won't even remember me walking by.

My mom was in the kitchen cooking dinner. That night was like every other night; fried potatoes and a pot of beans is what we would be eating. My mother always tried to make the best dinner she could, but most of our money went to buy the beer that my father was addicted to. That night was a special night; we would have chicken to go with our dinner.

My Mother was a good cook, but she cooked as most Southerners'; a pound of grease to fry everything we ate. Something about the grease frying would fill the air with an aroma that was like no other. It smelled wonderful. Add that to an iron skillet filled with Chicken and it was like Heaven.

I look up at my mother and smile. She is such a sweet lady and I always thought she was one of the most beautiful ladies I have ever seen. Her heritage is that of a Cherokee Indian. Her Grandmother was an Indian squaw and was bought by a mill worker somewhere in Wyoming. Through the years their children had continued to show the features of the Cherokee within their faces. My mother was no exception. Her hair was black and her eyes were blue, she looked like a native Angel. But she was worn out and tired. She worked hard everyday, then came home and took care of me, my sister and my drunken father. She did not drink, in fact she hated it. Although she insisted one day she was going to buy herself a bottle of Jack Daniels and drink it all in one night. I often wondered why she would say that, but now I understand that in her own way she thought it would somehow get back at my dad for all that he had done to her.

It is time to eat dinner, so I walk through my room and toward the bathroom. I need to wash my hands before we eat. I peak over my father as I pass by. He is staring at me. My heart plummets into my stomach as he demands me to pull my pants down. I stop and stare at him. Had I heard him correctly? I was dumbfounded. Why would a grown man ask a child to do such a thing? I continue to stare at him in disbelief.

As I child I felt I should do as told, but deep my heart or maybe it was my soul; I knew it was wrong.

Defiance in my house meant you would be spanked, so I was confused.

Within seconds my Mother came storming out of the kitchen holding a cast iron skillet filled with fried potatoes in her hand. I looked up at her. It is obvious that she had heard what he had demanded. She had saved me.

After instructing me to go sit on the porch for a few minutes, she walked over to where my dad was sitting. It was only seconds after I closed the front door behind me that yelling could be heard coming from within the living room. I sat on the porch and cried. Why had my dad asked me to do such a thing? I was eleven years old and I was his daughter. Tears streamed down my face, like a summer thunderstorm. I could not control my emotions. I was scared. I was angry. I no longer trusted my father.

The yelling suddenly ceased. I heard the front door open. I glanced up. It was my mother. Her face was emotionless. I was told to go into the kitchen, get dinner, eat, take a shower then go to bed. Afraid to face my father, I kept my head faced down while I walked through the living room. It was silent, and the TV was no longer on. I peaked up; he was no longer in the living room.

That night I did not feel like eating but I did not want to hurt my mother's feelings so I ate slowly; never eating very much. My mother, sitting next to me, looked out into nothingness.

I wanted to ask her why my dad would ask such a thing from me, but I was afraid to ask. Besides she was not saying anything, so she obviously did not want to talk what had happened. The room remained eerily silent, with not a word being spoken between us. Within her eyes she looked saddened but it was hard to tell because she would not look at me.

I got up from the table, took my plate and washed it in the sink. I wanted to let her know that I loved her so I kissed her on the cheek then scurried my way to the bathroom to take a shower.

I did not realize that what had happened had affected me as much as it did. That was until I got into the bathroom.

As I undressed I became embarrassed. I was young and until that point I never really paid attention to my changing body.

I felt disgusting and dirty, but not dirty like "I had playing all day and I am now dirty" type dirty, like I did something wrong that warranted my dad's request. I began to cry again. I believed that is why my mother had not talked to me; she was angry with me. My body was changing and somehow I had flaunted myself. That was only explanation I could come up with.

That night I did not take a shower. I couldn't stand looking at myself. I wanted my body to be covered.

Everyone went to bed early that night, so by the time I was done in the bathroom my sister was already in bed.

I had two stuffed animals that always sat on my bed. One was a tiny little orange mouse and the other was a stuffed panda that had rabbit fur on its back. Every night I slept with them; they were like a security blanket to me.

I was a naive child and felt that I had to always keep them faced up or they would suffocate. I remember always placing them a certain way on my bed and when I slept with them I made sure that their noses were not covered. That night I snuggled them next to me as close as I could, ignoring their possible suffocation.

My sister and I slept in a bunk bed, my

bed was on top. I felt save up there, but it did not stop me from crying that night. My sister asked me what was wrong many times, but I never answered her. I was too embarrassed to tell her what had happened.

I am uncertain if this was truly the next day or not. I remember the incident, but do not remember when it happened.

The next day when my mom dropped me off for school, I did not give her a kiss like I usually did. Due to the fact that she never spoke to me about what had happened, I was confused and afraid that she had blamed me for what happened the night before. In fact I felt that both my parents had, because I did not see my dad that morning as I usually did; so I felt that he too was avoiding me.

My day at school was like every other day. I was not liked by the other children, so I really never had any friends to play with. I never could understand why the other children hated me so, but sometimes I thought it was because we were poor and my clothing was not as nice as theirs. In fact they were hand-me-downs from my sister.

I spent the day like most others. I walked into school, ate breakfast then went to my classroom. There was never a problem until lunch time came around. That is when trouble always found me.

That day I had ate lunch and went outside to play. My favorite thing was to play on the monkey bars. I always played alone and never bothered anyone.

You watch shows on TV and there always seems to be one person that liked to bully someone else. That was a girl named Shawna. Her family had a lot of money so she was very popular. I was her favorite person to pick on.

I was a small girl; short for my age; always had been. I could always tell by the way she is looked at me if today was another day she wanted to pick a fight with me. That day was one of those days. Within minutes she was standing front of me trying to get me to fight with her. Her reasons for wanting whoop on me were always invalid.

I was the girl that she knew would

not fight back. I had no reason to want to fight anyone; not even in self defense.

She started saying mean things to me; calling me names as she usually did, then she swung and hit me across the face. Usually I would just walk away, but not that day. I was in a bad mood. I hit her back. The fight begins. For once I am getting an upper hand on her and taking my wrath of fury out on her.

After only a few of my hits connect with her body her friends joined in and before I knew it I was being held down on the grass by her friends while she wailed into my stomach, and my face with her fists. I could move. I could no longer defend myself. More of her friends joined in and began ripping clumps of grass from the ground and throwing it in my face. Grass and dirt got into my eyes. I could no longer see. I could not scream because the children were throwing grass into my mouth. I had no other choice but to lie there and take the beating that I was receiving and hope for an Adult to stop the fight.

I was not released until the school

bell rang. No adult had seen the fight. Although I was bruised and scratched I didn't care. Another day... another beating. I brushed myself off and went to class.

I had always had a slight slur to my speech so I always hated when the teacher would ask me to read. The other kids always fun of me because of the way I talked. *Baby talk* is what they would call it. I tried to not speak in such a manner, but for years I had problems saying my R's and S's. I knew I sounded funny and I hated the way I talked. But I could not help it. That day was not my day to read, so I able to avoid any further teasing.

The day went by fast and I had no more incidents with the gang of kids that had hurt me so bad earlier that day. That I was thankful for.

I had to walk home that day. My Mother was working so there was no one to pick me up. My sister went to a different school so there is no one to walk with, just me, myself and I. I always hate to walk home. My school was on the other side of town, so I had to walk across the main casino strip to get home. I liked the lights that were on the casinos, but what I didn't like were the drunken people that were walking up and down the streets. They scared me.

My legs were tired from the fight earlier so I walked slowly. There was a house of nuns that I believe was across the street from our house. I always liked to stop and look at the house. It gave me peace.

My memory fades for a while at this point. I can not say if was days, weeks nor months after the first incident with my father, but I can say this is when I realized my life would be tortured by men.

We still lived in Las Vegas and once again I was walking home from school. I was just few blocks from my house when a man slowly pulled up in a car. I can't remember the car, but I can remember the man. He looked to be in his 30's, his hair was blonde and long and kind of wavy. When he finally stopped the car he was right beside me.

He yelled to me from the driver's side of the car. He had rolled down the passenger window so it was easier for me to hear him. I reluctantly walked closer to his car to see what it was that he needed. I looked in. He was not wearing pants and he had private parts in his hand moving his hand in such a way that he was pleasuring himself. He was disgusting. Fear overtook me and I began to run. I never looked back to see he if he had left. I continued to run until I was home.

Once again a feeling came about me. Something I did warranted this man to act the way he did. I felt that I was doing something wrong. But once again, I didn't know what it was. I never told anyone what happened that day or at least I don't think I did. I always feared that I would be blamed and in some manner get into trouble.

Chapter 3
California 1980's

My memories fade once again, bringing me to a few years later. I am now in my teenage years. I am thirteen to be exact. We had moved from Las Vegas to live with my Uncle and his family. Work had run out in Las Vegas so my Father and my Uncle have decided to start a masonry business in Santa Ana California. My uncle has a nice house, a wonderful wife and four children. Because there is not enough room inside the house my Mother and Father will live in a small trailer in the backyard and my sister and I will share a room with two of my cousins.

I do not really remember my

Parents staying in this trailer; this was told to me.

I can not say for sure if all got along, because I really don't know, but I think we did.

I was the smallest, but not the youngest of the family so I was the choice of the others to pick on.

At first their little jokes were innocent, but then they got worst and down right mean. They started off by doing such things as putting something disgusting in my food when I was not looking or hiding things from me. I guess I thought this was okay because we were young and we were all doing this to one another. But then I guess they got bored of that and decided they needed to bring the torture up a notch.

One day while I was in the shower, one of my cousins came into the bathroom without me knowing it and took my clothes and the towel I was going to use to dry off with. When I got out of the shower I had nothing to cover up with.

They had left the door unlocked

and as soon as they heard the shower turn off they ran into the bathroom and pulled me out. I had not a stitch of clothing on. I tried to fight but there were two of them. I can't say who it was, because all I remember is that there were always two of them, maybe three.

They pulled me down the hallway to the front door. I remember I was crying and scared. I did not know what was going to happen.

To my horror, they opened the front door and threw me outside. The door was locked behind me so I had no way to get in. All that was keeping the outside world from seeing me in my nakedness was a block wall. I pounded on the door for what seemed to be hours. No one inside cared and all I could hear was the laughter from the girls inside as they mocked me.

I had no other choice, I would have to hop the wall and run to the back side of the house and hope that a window or the backdoor was unlocked.

I peeked through the holes that the wall possessed and looked around as best I could. It was early in the day so I was hoping that the people that lived around us were in their homes or at work. The street looked free of any others, so I felt confident that I could make it around the house unnoticed.

Hurrying as fast as I could I climbed the eight foot wall. I can still feel the roughness of the brick as it scratched my skin, causing me to suffer scraps and bruises in my inner thighs and sides. I ran to the back fence. I had forgotten that the gate was always kept locked, so I would have to climb a seven foot chain-link fence. I received more cuts, more bruises.

I tried every window on that side of the house and the back door. They had not forgotten to lock anything. I was hostage to their joke and could not get in.

Their laughter was heard coming from everywhere within the house as they ran from window to window, opening the windows, then closing them, teasing me.

I had been standing outside, naked and embarrassed for a while and I was nowhere closer to getting inside. Suddenly I heard a car pull into the driveway. It was either one of our parents or my oldest cousin. In my heart I hoped that it is my Mother. She needed to see what was happening so that she could put a stop to it.

Unexpectedly the window beside me opened and clothing was thrown toward me. Although I wanted whoever it is that had came home to see the truth, I was worried that it could be my dad, my uncle or the only other boy that lived there. All of which I did not want to expose myself too. I hurried and put my clothing on.

I walked over to the backdoor as I heard the lock being unlatched. The door opened. I walked inside at the same time my mother walked in. I was crying. But my tears were that of anger and not sadness. The girls had embarrassed me to the point that all I felt toward them was the utmost hatred.

I tried to explain to my mom what had happened. The others come in and said that I was making it all up and that they did throw me out but I had my clothes on and it was for only a minute. My plea for justice was ignored. They had won and I had lost.

I never could understand why my Mother did not believe me. Sometimes I think that she was so tired that she chose to ignore it.

For the next couple of months my torture was repeated. It came to a point that I was afraid to take a shower anymore. Locking the door did no good; they had figured out how to unlock it from the outside. There was no reason to tell anyone anymore, no one believed me anyway. No one ever believed anything I said and I don't know why.

The people who did this to me still think it is funny to talk about. In fact they bring it up all too often. To this day it still embarrasses me when they speak of it. The worst is when they talk about it to my friends or my children. I want to tell them how I truly feel about it, but I know it will just start an argument so I keep how I feel to myself.

Months down the road I was

asked to go for a ride with a person that I will not state. He had always treated me nicely so I decided that I would go with him, besides he has never done anything to me that would make me feel any different.

All we would be doing would be going to the store. He was bored and said that he would like the company. We got into the car. He had a cool car and I was but a teen, so I was excited to be riding in it. I felt special. No one was ever allowed in his car, but I was invited to go along with him.

We never made it to the store; instead he drove me to a dark park. I am not sure where the park was, but it was dark and desolate. I did not like where we were and I got a bad feeling that something terrible was about to happen to me. He parked toward the back of the park where it was blackest. My stomach began to sicken.

After turning off the car he rested his hand on my thigh, leaned forward and tried to kiss me. This man was much older then I and I was a child.

I leaned as far back as I could; my body trembled in fear. I did not want to kiss him and surely did not want to do anything else that he might have had on his mind.

Why was he doing this? Why was my young life continued to be tortured so?

I wanted to run back home, but I didn't know where I was. I had not lived in California for long, so I did not know my way around.

As my panic grew, he leaned in again. His body was now next to mine. He placed is disgusting lips on mine and kissed me. My heart raced, not with excitement, but with fear. What was going to happen next? Wasn't he afraid that I would say something to someone? Or did he already know that no one would believe me anyway?

He seemed amused by the fear I was feeling, it was like it fueled his desire to have me.

Suddenly there was a tapping sound coming from the driver-side window. He leaped away from me and looked out of the window. It was a police officer. He wanted to know what we were doing there so late in the evening. The man explained to him that my family had recently moved there and that he was only showing me around. I sat silent afraid that if I told the truth to the officer that I would anger the man and that somehow he would get his revenge on me.

I am uncertain if the officer believed the man's story, but he instructed him to take me home and to leave the park right away. On the way home I was told by the man that he was just joking around and that I should not say anything. I knew he was lying, he knew exactly what he was doing and that more then likely he had already planned out what he was going to do. I bit my tongue and kept his dirty little lie a secret.

I lived in a house where I felt like I could not trust anyone. The young girls that lived there were torturing me with their pranks and more then ever I was scared of any man.

Our family moves out of my Uncles house a few months later. We don't move far though, just around the corner. I can relax. I will not have to suffer the torture of being thrown outside with no clothes. I am finally free of the pain that they were putting upon me; both physically and mentally.

A year had gone by and I was now in eighth grade. Soon I would be in high school. Things were better for me. I had my own room. But I remember I did not stay in that room often; usually I stayed with my sister in hers. I don't really remember why, but I do have my suspicions.

I am still short for my age, but I am beginning to blossom into a young woman. I have the typical 80's look. This included the big hair and enough makeup on to make a clown jealous. This should have been the best years of my life. The life of a teenager, but the change that was happening to me would prove to be a destination for abuse.

At this point I have become distant from my family. I have been hurt by them and no longer trust very many people. I have made new friends at school, although I am far from being the most popular girl in class.

It is late one night and I am sitting in the living room. My mother is in bed and so is my sister. My Father comes in and sits beside me. He has been working all day and his hands are cut and chapped from the cement that they use. Every since that day in Las Vegas I continued to feel uncomfortable around him. But since he was my dad I forgave him for what he had asked me to do that day.

I continued to sit with him and for the first time in years we were talking. I look over at the lotion that he is using and ask him what it is. He tells me that it is a great lotion that helps his hands "Corn Huskers" was the name.

I will never ever forget the name of neither that lotion nor what the bottle looked like.

He asked if I would like to try some of it. I say sure. By this time I am sitting on the floor with my legs out in front of me watching TV. It is summer, so I am wearing shorts.

He came and sat next to me and put some of the lotion in his hands. I tell him that I can do it myself but he insists that he puts some on my feet. Being a naive child, I allow him to do so. I did not like the way it felt to have his hands against my bare skin. It felt unnatural and wrong.   I try to get up, but he holds me down and begins to rub the lotion up my leg to my inner thigh. Before I can fight my way away from him, he already taken all my trust and respect I had left for him and chewed it up and had spit it on the floor.

To my horror he was touching me with his disgusting hands in a place that a young woman my age should never had be touched and defiantly not by her dad. I kicked him as hard as I could and then ran to the bathroom and began crying.

Why did these men feel that they could touch me in the way that they were?

My mother who was once asleep heard my cries and inquired to what is going on. My father was outside the bathroom door apologizing to me and lying to her. He told my mom that he said something that made me mad. Once again I remained silent.

At that point it was more that I feared men and what would happen to me, if I was to ever tell. If they were willing to do this to me, what would they do to me if I told? The only thing I could see in my future was more pain more torture if I ever told their secrets.

I would like to say that my horror stops there, but it does not. I was a target for men and this point I was starting to believe that somehow unconsciously I was doing something that made men feel that they were allowed to treat me in such a manner that they need not respect me or my body. In that year, I was attacked one other man. He was a young school boy from school. I was going to my friend's house to visit her. That day I had decided to take a short cut through the desolated school. It was the weekend so no one would be at the school. They never locked it or so I thought.

What I didn't know was that I was being followed by one the boys that is in my class. He had seen me walking down the street and for some reason decided to follow me, or maybe it was his plan all along to do what he did. Maybe he was just waiting for the perfect moment.

The back fence was not locked, so I continued through the school with confidence. One more fence was the only thing stopping me from freedom. The fence at the other end of the school was locked. I would have to go back to where I came from and walk around.

I had been walking for a while so I had decided to rest for a minute before I walked back through the long corridor. Within seconds a young man walked up behind me. He was young like me; thirteen years old, but he was a strong boy; one of the jocks of the school. He held me down and tried to rip my shirt off. He said that he had heard that I was a whore and that I would have sex with anyone. I never knew where that rumor came from. I did not have a boyfriend and I surely had not had sex with anyone. I hadn't even had a kiss before.

I don't remember how I got away, but I do remember him hitting me with a tennis racket across my mouth, causing my bottom tooth to shatter.

I did tell on this boy. My mother and I and the principal of the school had a meeting with the boy.

Once again I would be left looking like the fool.

He lied and said that I hit him that is why he hit me with the racket. He denied the rest and was allowed to leave the office. The only prove I had been hurt was my word and the broken tooth in my mouth. Obviously it was not enough to warrant any kind of justice for me. I do think my mom believed me, but I can not be for certain, because nothing was further said about the situation. I was taken to the dentist and a cap was put on the broken tooth.

Because he was one of the most popular boys in school, rumors scattered throughout the school fast. I was quickly hated by most, and my remaining school year was spoiled.

Chapter 4
July 1981

July of 1981 is a memory that I am not sure truly is a memory. I have been told this story so many times that my doctor says that it might be a forced memory. He says this because I can not pull out any other memory from this time, besides what I have been told. But it is a lovely memory so I like to pretend that I really remember that weekend.

We had moved again. Now we live close to Disneyland.

My sister has had a boyfriend for a while now so she is rarely home. I always thought it was because she was to busy with her new love and that she only wanted to be with him.

I stay away from my dad as much as possible and lock my bedroom door at night. My sister shares a room with me and when she is home she likes the door locked also. It wasn't until a few years ago that I found out why. She too had been molested by my father. This saddened me. As young women we had both been afraid to tell what was happening; we didn't even trust to tell one another.

I always say that July 4th 1981 was the day I was saved. My sister was to go with her friend for a camping trip with her friend's family. Because my sister's boyfriend could not go she did not go and instead I went.

We had been there for about a day when her friend and I decided to walk around. We were bored and needed something to do. It was hot out so we decided to wait till dusk when it was a little bit cooler. It was small campground with a street that looped around it. I remember the street, but that is all I remember about the campsite.

We had only been walking a few

minutes when we suddenly heard a revving engine behind us. I turned around. It was two guys in a small red truck. I did not pay attention to what they looked like; I did not care. It was a man and to me he was being inappropriate. I flipped them off.

The next day it was so hot outside that the only thing there was to do was to play in the river. My friend and I walked down the river back until we found a spot that the river ran slowly. It was the perfect place to cool off. But there was one problem; there was already two guys swimming there and they were jumping off the rock that we wanted to hang out on.

After deliberation my friend and I decided to stay.

At first the guys ignored us and I could not figure out why. But then after a while we all began to swim together. I was unaware that is was the same two guys we had seen in the truck the day before. The same two guys I flipped off and that is why at first they were ignoring us; they were offended by the rudeness I had shown them.

After an hour or so, the one that I thought was cute finally confessed that he was the one I had shown my middle finger too. We all got a laugh out of it and the rest of the day we had a great time.

Later that night after we had ate dinner with my friends family we decided to walk around to see if we could find the guys camp. It was only a few campsites beside us. We hung out for hours there, talking to the guys. In the time that we were there I lied and told the one that I liked that I was 18 years old. He was 20 years old and I liked him so much that I did not want him to know that I was truthfully only 14 years old.

We were leaving the next day and I feared that I would never see him again, so I took a necklace off of his neck and told him that he would have to come see me if he ever wanted it back.

What I do remember about the weekend that I met him was that he never tried to do anything to me. So much so that I one point I thought that maybe he did not like me in the way I liked him. At this point I was confused about men. I thought if a man liked you it was normal to force themselves on you. This man never did, so I was confused.

To my surprise John; the man I had met at the river, called me the following day and we made plans for him to come visit me the weekend coming. I was excited to see him again but I was living a lie. He believed me to be older then I was. I had to tell him the truth.

I called him and told him that I was only 14 years old. Later in years he confessed to me that he thought I was telling him that because I did not want to see him. We both laugh at it now. Unfortunately my memories end here and do not reemerge until fourteen years later.

We married on September 7th 1981. By this time we had one child; a little boy named Jeffery. He turned one year old six days before our wedding.

Unfortunately I do not remember our wedding and for some reason have very few pictures of that day. I can say that by looking at the pictures that I do have it is obvious that my husband and I were very happy and very much in love.

I wish I could remember that day. A women's wedding day is always a day that she treasures. But for me it is another memory lost.

Chapter 5

March 25th 1995 (Reborn)

Exhausted, and sore, I opened eyes and noticed that I was in a room that was unfamiliar to me. I looked around. The room was bright and unwelcoming. Sitting in a chair next to my bed was a man that seemed to have been there for a long time. His hair was tangled and his face showed signs of stress. He was sleeping, but his sleep was not that of peace. He seemed as if a nightmare was haunting him.

After I stared at him for a few moments I decided it was best to let him sleep as the dark circles under his eyes indicated to me that he had not been sleeping well.

Quietly, I slipped to the edge of the bed, wrapped the hospital gown that I was wearing around me so that I was not exposed to anyone that may have been looking. My stomach was hurting so I walked with my body hunched over; I felt as if I could not stand upright. As I passed the man in the chair, I walked slowly ensuring that I did not disturb him. The bathroom door was just on the other side of the bed, so I was certain I could make it there on my own.

I could only take small steps at a time. My back began to scream in pain. I could not continue walking in the scrunched position that as I was. As I stood straight, a pain overtook my lower stomach causing me to immediately bend back over. My hands were sore and bruised, which only allowed me to only put minimal pressure onto my newly found pain. Tears filled my eyes, as the pain became overwhelming, but with determination I slowly made my way to the bathroom.

Although I had to use the restroom, I was more interested in seeing why my body was hurting so badly. After what seemed an eternity I finally made it to the bathroom door. I was out of breath and in extreme pain, so I stopped for just a second and looked at myself. The vision in the mirror had deceived me so I continued on with my mission as now I had to use the bathroom more then ever before. Ever before? Ever before?

I had no idea if I had ever had to use the bathroom this bad before, because I don't remember ever using a bathroom.

I have no answer. My mind is blank. I sat quietly and tried to think of anything; something that would explain why I felt so lost and confused.

As I sat there a vision of what I had just seen in the mirror flooded my mind. My mind had accepted the vision as truth, whereas every bit of my soul and heart mind refused to accept what I had seen.

My body was sore and weak, but I ignored the pain and scurried my way back to the mirror. I remember staring in that mirror for the longest time. I was in disbelief. Who was that horrible monster staring back at me?

As where you would think a vibrant 29 year old would be, was a hideous creature whose tongue had been chewed to the point that it possessed bite marks on either side of it and swollen to extent that it would no longer fit in my mouth. My eyes, once blue, were encased in blood; not even allowing the white areas to shine, as they were filled with the red serum also.

I looked closer as deviance of the mirror continued to haunt me. My face, mutilated and swollen showed only the multiple colors of purple, blue, red and yellow as the bruises had taken over my skin. I closed my teary eyes, and then opened them again, hoping that the deception I was seeing would disappear when I reopened them. The horror of what stood in front of me never faded.

I walked back over to my bed and crawled back under the covers, in hopes that the warmth would offer me some kind of comfort. It didn't. I continued to ponder so many questions.

The man in the chair stretched his muscles, then stood up and leaned over and kissed my cheek. Within his words of love he called me "Doll Face."

My heart began to beat in fear. Who was this man and why was he is kissing me. My anguish was apparent by my lack of response. He quickly sat down and tried to explain to me what had happened.

His story was that of complete horror and at first I found it hard to believe. After explaining to me in great detail what had happened seven days before, I stared at him in disbelief. What he told me was incomprehensible to me. I tried to un-cloud my mind so I might be able to remember an inkling of what he was telling me.

He had explained to me that I was pregnant, but his words seemed defiant to me. I didn't remember being pregnant. I felt my stomach; it was sore and hurt to touch. I tried to voice my concerns but my tongue was swollen making it impossible to talk. But the man seemed to be able to understand me.

He assured me that what I had heard him say is true. I was pregnant and in fact had given birth to a little girl.

I was afraid to ask him who he was, but I had no other choice; I had to know who he was. My self conscious is telling me that he must be my husband because I can not understand why anyone else would call me by "Doll Face" unless they were my husband or possibly a boyfriend.

Through my slurred and stuttered words, I did just that. I asked him who he was. Immediately the man sat back in his chair and stared at me; silence overtaking the room. With that one question I felt as if I had taken his spirit and ripped from inside of him.

The man gave me a look of concern and I could tell by his expression he was mortified that I had asked such a question.

After looking at me for a while in confusion he explained that he was my husband and that had been married for ten years and that the baby I had gave birth to was in NICU.

At that point I didn't know what NICU was. Even though he had explained everything to me, my brain was still swollen so his words did not mean a thing to me. My comprehension level was null and void.

Questions ran through my head, ignoring the answers that he had already told me. I was uncertain why I was there, who I was, and how is it that out of everything that was going on that I was able to remember him as my husband, bet yet not remember his at all. Did I believe him because there was no one else there to tell me any different, or did a part of me remember him?

Our conversation was interrupted when a man in white jacket; a man I had never seen before entered the door. He walked over to me and put a cold metal device on my chest and proceeded to, what I believe to do is check my heartbeat.

He talked to me like he had known me for a while. But I did not know him.

I try to speak again. I have a lot questions that I needed answers to. But once again my voice found it hard to escape past my tongue that was housing my entire mouth. After trying many times, I realized that I was making no sense at all. Both men continued to stare at me with confusion upon their face.

The man in the white jacket could tell that I was becoming more distressed then ever so he explained to me as best as he could that I had a disease called *Eclampsia.* He further explained that from the disease I had became extremely sick. I had gone into grand-mal seizures and was taken to the hospital. The baby was taken by c-section and is now in NICU. She is doing okay, in fact we both seem to be doing okay, although he admits there was a moment that he thought we both were not going to live.

I stared at that man, emotionless.

He looked stunned by my reaction. He is concerned that I do not remember, but says that he is sure that my memory loss is temporary.

At that point I didn't remember

any of it. In fact I didn't even know my name. No one had spoken my name. I began to wonder if what he was saying true. Would I remember and if so when. But more then anything I wanted someone to say my name. I had to know what it was. I was afraid to ask.

I don't know why I was afraid to ask, but I was.

I wanted to scream "What did you say my same was?" But I remained silent.

The man left the room, with unanswered questions. I could understand how it was that I had a disease and because of that disease they had to take the baby early. But why couldn't I remember anyone including myself and why am I am beaten and bruised so badly.

They explained that they had to take her by c-section, but no one explained why my tongue is swollen, why my eyes are red or why I had bruises all over my body.

The rest of the day my room was overtaken with people coming in and out, all of which seemed excited to see me awake and somewhat alert. The problem being, I didn't know any of them. To me they were strangers I had no memory of.

The day had turned to night and I was tired. Everyone had left for the day and that I was thankful for. I was tired both mentally and physically and needed to rest. The man that was my husband checked to see if I needed anything and once he felt like I was comfortable he informed me that he was going to go see the baby. Cheyenne Autumn was her name.

My heart was sad because I had been told that I could not see the baby until I was discharged from the hospital and that could be a few more days. I graciously told him that I would be fine, never showing him the true depression that was wheeling inside of me.

After few minutes of being alone in the room I decided that I would go back into the bathroom, I had to know if the reflection in the mirror I had seen earlier would be the same.

I knew it was going to hurt to get out of bed and that I probably should not do it alone, but my curiosity of what happened wouldn't let me rest. Maybe seeing myself again would spark some type of memory. With my beaten and sore body somehow I managed to get to the mirror a little quicker this time. I glanced into the reflection and to my horror, the image from earlier was still there. I cried as memories of what had happened flooded my mind like someone had just opened the gates of Hell upon me.

My eyes burned and the salt from the tears attacked the cuts on my face, causing pain. But I could not stop crying. I looked like a monster. As I continued to look in the mirror, memories continued to flood my mind. I remembered what had happen that brought me to where I was.

This memory continues to haunt me to this day and it is hard for me to write about it. But I will share with you what I experienced, what I saw and the life that I lost.

I had woken up on the 24th of March, not feeling so well. I called the doctor and was informed by him that I should eat potato, as the description of the pulsating light in my eyes was indication that I needed potassium. My mother lived with us then so I remember talking to my mom and asking her if she thought any kind of potato would work. After discussing it for a few minutes I decided to bake a potato in the microwave and eat it. The rest of the day I can't remember, leaving me only with the vision of midnight that night. I had woken up with such a terrible headache that my pain refused to let me rest. I went to the refrigerator, got something to drink and then went back to my bedroom and sat on the edge of the bed. The headache would not subdue.

Within minutes of my restlessness my husband woke up and asked me what was wrong. I had explained to him about the pain in my head and how I wasn't quite feeling right. Because of the pregnancy I had not been feeling well for the past few days, he decided that it was just another episode of me feeling sick and nothing to really worry about. After instructing me to drink my water then lay back down, he went into the kitchen himself to get a refreshing drink of ice cold water.

Never did he expect to return and witness what he was about to encounter. As sitting in the middle of the bed was me on my knees, my hands supporting my body in front of me.

I was screaming for him to help me as I continued to beg him to stop them from taking me away.

Above my bed was a vision of a bright light encircled by clouds with the faces of loved ones that had passed away. Their hands spread towards me, inviting me to go towards the light, but my mind refused to let go. I refused to go. I had people here on earth that love me and I love them, it was not my time. They could not have me!

I continued chant-like repeating to my husband that I did not want to go. My pleading words echoed through the room like a skipping record. I could not stop. They were getting closer and I knew it was not my time to leave. I could not leave.

The light continued to get brighter and the people closer. I was loosing the battle; I would soon be theirs. For what seemed like eternity I continued to point up toward the ceiling; the vision of the people for only me to see. My husband had no idea what was happening, nor what I was speaking of.

Afraid of what was going on my husband pulled me into his arms and set me on the side of the bed, trying to snap me out of the unknown trance I was in.

The room, now silent of my words, he desperately tries to bring me back.

In body I was there with him, but my mind was no longer there. I could see him but I could not tell if he was real.

Without warning I looked over at him, my eyes that of emptiness, shed a tear as my head proceeded to jerk from side to side with such violence that it is incomprehensible to why my neck did not snap.

I began screaming at him to make it stop. But he couldn't. He could not stop the violence that the disease was putting on me.

My tongue was being chewed by my own teeth and I couldn't stop it, I had no control of my movements. The torment was horrific as it shot waves of pain through my mouth, as my teeth took big chucks out of my tongue. Blood began squirting from my mouth as I devouring my own tongue.

Not truly thinking about what he was about to do, my husband stuck the side of his hand in my mouth, trying to relieve my tongue from anymore abuse.

His hand took a thrashing as my teeth sunk deep into his skin. I tried to make it all stop, but my arms were now out of control also, swinging around in such an uncontrollable force that he too was now taking a beating. He refused to let me hurt myself anymore and hung onto me as tight as he could. The violence lingered on as my muscles ripped from being held hostage. My husband thought he was doing the right thing by holding me down, but what was actually happening was that my body was in convulsions and because he was holding me down my muscles were being pulled and ripped.

I would like to say that the convulsion only lasted a few seconds, but it lasted about five minutes. The room suddenly went dark and my body limp. He released me and I fell to the bed. I was gone. The light that I had seen earlier was the one that was winning the battle. The light faded leaving lost in the dark.

I saw nothing, just blackness as it engulfed my body. I was left with the lasting sound of my husband screaming "No!"

I wanted to look around but my mind was no longer working and would not allow my eyes to open. The man screamed again, his voice of desperation caught my attention. The darkness began to fade as a strange mist took over the hollowness that I was feeling. I looked through the darkened haze and saw the face of my dear departed Father. He was instructing me to leave the darkness. I was no longer feeling the pain that I had been. I was at peace and no longer wanted to leave.

The serene place that I was in was dark with only one bright light in the distance. I felt welcomed. Suddenly the brightness faded as I felt my body being shaken. I heard a voice then another. They are all screaming my name. Shawna is my name. Shawna is my name.

They wanted me to come back. But where was that. Back to where. I felt safe where I was.

My body was shaken violently again, causing my consciousness to become more aware of what was going on. The place I so desperately was craving was heaven. But for me to stay there meant the death of me and the loss of a Mother, a wife, a sister and daughter, to people I really loved. I couldn't do that to them. I had to leave the place that was offering me the peace of mind I have been looking for all my life.

I tried to stay coherent, but my body was weak and sick and quickly faded again, leaving me with the only the memory of two men desperately screaming within an ambulance, trying to keep my attention.

As my soul continued to fade in and out, I asked in desperation where my husband was. If this was my last moment on Earth, I wanted it to be with him.

I was told that he was in the car behind us. Although I never got an explanation to as why; I was told that he was not allowed to ride in the ambulance.

My heart saddened as more then anything at that moment I wanted him by my side. We had been together since I was 14 years old; he was my best friend. I needed the safety of his arms around me.

Blackness overtook me once again as I hear the men that I had been talking to scream. They sounded desperate and scared for my life. They needed to get me to the hospital right or they would loose the battle they were fighting to keep me alive.

With my eyes, heavy as two boulders, I tried to look up to ensure the man that I was going to be okay. I could see the men, I can hear the men, but my consciousness was no longer there. I could not speak. I could not move. I faded into the darkness again.

"We have to take the baby," Would be the next words I heard. "The baby may not make it, but if we don't take her now, you will die again and we fear we will not be able to bring you back this time. Your brain to swollen, we have no choice."

Trying to fight the hollowness of the haze that was trying to overtake my soul, I looked up. It was my doctor that was speaking to me.

The next thing I remember was a light appearing above me once again and the room exploding in panic as every nurse and Doctor proceeded to bring me back from death. One nurse repeating my name over and over again as she tried to keep me with them.

Sometimes I still can hear her

desperate cries.

The days leading from that time to the point I am now, are lost. I would learn later that I was in a coma for seven days. Six of those days in ICU. My brain had swollen to the point that my body had shut down. They explained it as it was the way my body could heal itself.

As I snapped out of the trance the memories had put me in, I realized that was why I looked as I did. I had experienced more then one person should ever and all within hours of a one night, died three times and by the graze of god was allowed to live.

I looked at myself again. I could see myself so I knew I was alive, but I had to question myself, "If I was alive? Could someone that went through so much truly be alive?"

Tears filled my swollen eyes as I continued to wonder about my past live. The worst fear of all, was that so many people had came too see me that day, and I did not know who they were and I still didn't. When would those memories come back was all that I could wonder.

I stayed in that hospital room for four more days. Every day my husband stayed with me; only leaving for short periods of time to go see Cheyenne.

Because of what I had gone through; the nurses allowed him to stay overnight.

Chapter 6

It was finally the day I was to be released from the hospital. Although I was excited to be going home, I was terrified, because I still did not know where home was. I had been told that I had two young boys at home waiting to see me. One was ten and one was five.

All I could wonder was what would they think when they see the monster I had become. My eyes, still filled with blood, my tongue still swollen and my face overcome with bruises would put fear in their hearts; that I was sure of. The worst thought of all comes to mind. How do I pretend to know these children when in my heart I have no memory of them? Will they know I am lying or will they buy into my deceit?

It was sad to think about my two sons. They were innocent children whose lives would be affected by one incident.

I hadn't been able to see the baby yet, but I was excited to do so. I had been warned that she is tiny and that at first it may scare me. She was born one pound six ounces and had lost weight. In my mind I don't know what that meant. I had seen other women in the room with their babies and they look healthy to me. Is my daughter truly that much smaller then theirs?

After gathering my things and signing the papers necessary for my discharge I was sat in a wheel chair and brought to NICU. The room was white and unwelcoming and the first thing that you came in contact with was a large sink with soap and scrub brushes. My husband and I were instructed to scrub our hands with the hottest water we could stand and continue doing that for ten minutes. My skin, still bruised and sore screamed in agony, but I wanted to see my baby so I endured the pain.

My husband talked to me in a calm concerned manner; he wanted to make sure that I was prepared for what I was about to see. I could not understand the urgency in his voice. She was a baby, I was certain that they were over reacting and that she looked like any other baby.

I told him that I would be fine. I was certain that what I was about to see would not affect me.

Although he understood my apprehension, he continued to explain to me that she was not like the others I had seen. The baby was only the size of my hand, and she had numerous amounts of wires coming from her body that were hooked to various monitors.

I peeked in the window before we went in and seen about ten different small cribs where babies are laying peacefully sleeping. For some reason I didn't believe what he was telling me.

The babies I was seeing all seemed to be healthy and although a little smaller then the others they were not as tiny as he was describing.

The door opened and the nurse

escorts us in. The room was as uninviting as the first room I encountered. The loud sounds of monitors beeped and screamed throughout the room causing my heart to sadden instantly. I looked around at all the babies and wondered which one of them was my "Cheyenne". I looked up at John in confusion.

My husband turned the wheelchair and pushed me into an area that was housed by glass and sat alone. My heart dropped and tears instantly filled my eyes as I looked into the glass dome that my baby rested in.

She was the smallest baby I had ever seen. She did not look real. Her skin was so thin that you could see every blood vein in her body. She was naked because her skin was so delicate that the lightest of cloth would cause her to bruise. My heart was torn apart; I began to sob in sorrow. I would not be able to touch her. I would not be able to feel her delicate skin on mine. She was enclosed in glass and the only way she would feel the comfort of my touch was through a little hole. My skin covered in a protective plastic, she can not feel the loving touch of a mother or a father for a long time. This poor baby must remain in this glass tomb for months never knowing any kind of love. I wanted out of that room so badly that I could feel myself panicking. I could not handle seeing her like that anymore, but yet, I wanted so badly to tell her that I was there for her, and that I loved her.

John could see the sadness that had overtaken me and tried to make me feel better. He took my hand in his and held it tightly, then explained to me that they said that she was doing well and that she would be fine.

I continued to stare at her. My heart wanted to believe him but mind was telling me different. She had so many tubes hooked to her that it was impossible to find a pot on her body that was not hooked up to some sort of machine. But out of everything that she had hooked to her, there was one thing that bothered me the most and that was a tube that was placed her mouth and down her throat.

I asked what the tube is for and why did it remain there at all times. My husband explained to me that the tube allowed them to feed her. She was too little to suck on a bottle so they must force-feed her.

I wanted to scream and yell. Did I do something wrong that warranted this baby to be born so early and to have no other choice but to suffer so badly in her first months of her life? I felt helpless and uncertain why something, someone so innocent had to be so sickly. She was only seven days old and out of those seven days there had not been a day that this baby had felt peace and love. She was thrown in a glass covered crib and the only attention she got was is when a nurse or doctor comes to check on her. Our voices would be the only comfort that she would know for a long time.

John talked to the baby and she moved. Her eyes opened and for the first time since I had been in this room I come in terms that she was alive and she was my baby.

We sat for hours that day, talking with the baby and the nurses.

Chapter 7

When I returned home, it was exactly as I feared. I did not know my sons; I did not know my mom. I was living in a house of strangers and I was one of them.

People came to see me, all of which did not know what was going on in my head. I was so confused, so lost and I was afraid to ask for help.

I did a good job pretending for a while, but then my deception became evident.

Family would talk about the past and at first I could lie my way through the stories. I would listen to them and responded in such a manner that I would just agree with what they were telling me, although I did not know what they were talking about and the memories, no matter how hard I tried, would not come back. Soon after I began adding stories to go along with theirs. I thought what I was saying really happened, but none of it was true. No one said anything to me, although they had no idea what I was talking about. They continued in their deviance as I continued in mine. I guess they thought that it was I needed, where in reality I needed someone to tell me the truth. Soon, I began believing my own lies.

Some family friends would stop by. I would be told who was coming over and in my mind I knew who they were, that was until they walked through the door. I then had no idea. Who I pictured in my mind was never the person that walked in. It was like I would listen to others speak of the person, so I would get a vision of what I thought they looked like, but my visions were never right. I was lost in a world that I was only familiar with.

Things got complicated. Family and friends began telling my husband that I changed. No one knew the girl who came home from the hospital. They explained that girl as someone who was quiet and secluded and someone who did not talk much. During holiday dinners they said she would be the one that would sit in the corner and never talk to anyone. I tried to understand what they were talking about but I didn't know who that other person was. They said it was me, but I didn't know that girl. I only knew who I was now.

The person I had turned into was someone who loved to talk and to be with others. I believe what I was trying to do was to understand who they were. I wanted to get to know them again. I was not afraid of them, but I did worry that they were afraid of me. I don't say this because I was mean or nasty, I was no longer the girl they knew and I knew this frightened them.

Knowing how the felt, I soon after became distant. I feared that I was disappointing the people I once knew and loved. I could not be the person that they wanted back. I did not want to be the person that they knew. I wanted to be me, be who I was now.

I did not understand until years later that they too felt lost. They did not know who I was and so they did not know how to react around me.

Months went by and I did not see very many people besides who lived in my house. My mother, who had been staying with us, went to live with her sister in New Mexico. She said could not deal with what had happened. By this time she knew I did not know her like I should. I had confessed in her and told her that I did not remember anyone. I hurt her by doing that, but I did not know I was going to. She left because she could not deal with the fact that she had lost her daughter; not by death but by death of a memory.

I wish I could take back the fact I told my mom the truth. The look in her eyes was confusion. I could not tell if she believed me or if she thought that some odd reason I was making it up. Later I found out it was sadness.

It was hard dealing with

everything around me. The sad thing is I still don't remember my sons being there this entire time. I know they were. But thinking back to that time in my life, I don't remember them. Even today, I can not remember them being there.

Sometimes I wonder if it was because there was so much happening, so much confusion and pain in my life at that time that I don't remember them. Or if I want to pretend that those two small boys did not see what I was going through.

Cheyenne was three months old when my mom left. She was growing and was about 3lbs. They said it would be about a month and then she should be able to come home. She was no longer in the glass bubble; instead she is in a small crib. She was still skinny and fragile, but she was the cutest thing I had ever seen.

My leg had been hurting me for a while so I had decided to go to the doctor. The first doctor told me that I pulled a muscle and that I should go home and tries to stay off of my leg for a while. I did as I was told but the leg never got any better.

Three days later I had woke up and saw that the leg that had been bothering me was then two times the size of the other and it was purple. I called the doctor that I had seen during my pregnancy. He did not seem too concerned but said that I could come in so that he could look at it.

The pain was unbearable so my husband took off work so that he could take me to the doctor. I had been having episodes to where I would forget where I was and sometimes would stare out into the emptiness for moments at time; I wanted to talk to the doctor about this also. I could no longer drive, so my only way around was for husband to take me.

My leg was so swollen that it made it almost impossible to walk; it was even harder to get in the car, because my leg did not want to bend at the knee.

The doctor looked at my leg briefly and then left the room suddenly. After a few seconds he returned, panicked. He instructed me to go to the hospital and to get there right away. He had already called them and told them to admit me. There was no explanation to as why; he said that there was not time to explain, that he would explain later. The hospital was just across the way, so he instructed my husband to wheel me over in a wheelchair and not to let me walk.

Within an hour I was in a hospital bed and had an IV in my arm. The doctor came in shortly after and explained to me what had happened to my leg.

From the disease and the birth of my daughter I had gotten blood clots in my veins "Deep Vein Thrombosis" to be exact. They had to put me in the hospital because there was so many of them that they were afraid that they would dislodge from my leg at any moment and go to lungs or worst yet into my heart. They had to dissolve them with the medication they were giving me through the IV.

I was devastated. I had to spend another week in the hospital. During that time I would not be allowed to see my daughter. I had a fever and so therefore they were afraid that although my fever was not from a virus that I would transmit the fever to my daughter and that would not be good for her. My husband once again would have to see me suffer and worry about loosing me. I hated seeing him in such distress. This man had already been through so much and once again he would have to go though more emotional devastation.

For that entire week, my husband would go to work, come see me, and then go see the baby. He would stay late and barely sleep. He was so tired, so worried. I was sick again and the baby was still in NICU. He feared that he would loose his wife and one of his children if things did not get better for us.

Cheyenne was doing okay, but she still could not eat on her own. This was worrying the doctors. If she could not eat on her own, she would not be able to leave. She lost weight again and became anemic. They were afraid that they would have to give her a blood transfusion. My husband was the one who would have to make the decision. I was in so much pain that I could not comprehend anything more then the torture I was experiencing.

My husband felt that he had no other choice but to let them do as they felt best. He signed the papers to allow the blood transfusion.

To our delight a miracle happened the day the transfusion was to be done. She began to eat on her own so they decided to wait a few days more to see if her blood got better. It did. Her anemia went away. She would not have to get a blood transfusion.

A week later my blood had thinned enough that they said I could go home. I would have to go to the hospital everyday, twice a day to get a shot in my stomach of blood thinners. That was the only way they would let me leave. I wanted out of the hospital so we agreed to their request and I was finally discharged.

I was still in a wheelchair and would be for a while. I could not walk on my leg for months to come.

The first thing I wanted to do was

to go see Cheyenne. The day we were leaving one of the nurses from NICU came up and got me and my husband. She had good news.

After washing our hands we were brought inside the room. Cheyenne was now in one the bigger cribs. It had been three and a half months since she was born and now weighed 3.5lbs. She could be held. For the first time, my husband and I would hold our baby.

The nurse picked her up and set her in my lap first. She was still so tiny it scared me. I could not stop shaking. I was afraid I would drop her. I tried to hold her as long as I could but the fear in me won, so handed her to my husband for him to hold.

Instantly I started crying. The day had come that I had been waiting for and I could not do it. I could not hold her. I was scared of how small she was.

I watched in jealousy while my husband held her and talked to her. I was jealous because he did not let fear win over his love for her; something I could not do.

Chapter 8

Although I remained in a wheelchair, my husband and I would go see Cheyenne everyday. I was still frightened to hold her. Not so much because she was small, but because my episodes of unawareness were happening more often.

Today was the day that she was going to be going home. We were excited but yet we tried to hold our excitement in. We had been told a few times that she would be going home, but when the time came something always happened and she was not allowed to come home. But that day there was nothing stopping us. They baby was healthy and the discharge papers were signed by the doctor. Our baby would be going home. It would now be up to us to ensure her safety and health. That was a scary thought.

She was four months old and weighed four pounds, the required weight for discharge. My husband and I were excited. We stayed for eight hours holding her and waiting for the nurse to come in and say that we could go.

We had decided to get rid of all of our animals because we feared that the dander from their skin would affect her breathing. Some of the animals we had for years, but we did not want to take a chance that she would become ill. I will admit it saddened me to get rid of them, but when it came to her health I wanted to be extra careful.

The first couple of weeks that she was home my husband were so afraid that she would suffocate in her crib so he slept on the couch with her cradled in his arms. He would sleep like I had never seen anyone else sleep before. It was like he was always aware that she was in his arms. He never moved, not even a budge.

This was a hard time for my husband. I was to remain in the wheelchair until I felt like I could walk without pain. Because I was in the wheelchair we had to sleep in the living room. There was a step down to our bedroom and bathroom so it was easier to stay in the living room. I had to have a port-a- potty because I could not make it into the bathroom. The medicine that the doctor gave me caused horrible diarrhea so I constantly had to use it. I remember I felt so bad because my husband would have to change it. He never complained.

Months went by and although my memory did not return, things were looking better. My leg was still bigger then the other but the blood clots had dissolved. It hurt to walk and I could no longer walk very far, but after five months I was finally out of a wheelchair.

My husband had not worked very much because of me and my daughter so we were being evicted from our house.

We had missed rent and there was no one to help us.

We moved a couple of times because my daughter and I continued to need medical care, causing my husband to miss more work. She was hospitalized because of her lungs and I remained having medical issues.

I had begun seeing a neurologist because my episodes of unconsciousness were getting out of control.

I had been driving with the kids and all of a sudden I blacked out and almost ran the car into a telephone pole. It was time to find out what was going on.

The doctor did some tests and came to the conclusion that I was having petit-mal seizures. My brain was still swollen from the grand-mal seizures I had experienced. I could not take the medicine necessary to stop the seizures in fear that I would get blood clots again. Unless they became worst I would have to live with what was happening.

This decision did not come easy for the doctor but he said that the chance of blood clots forming again was greater then the chance of the seizures growing in intensity.

I saw the doctor for over a year. In that time I spoke with him about the memory loss I was experiencing. He did some tests and found out that not only was I suffering from long term memory loss but I was suffering minimally from short time memory loss. The short term memory could be being caused from the seizures, but the seizures seemed to be fading.

I was also told that day that after seven years, what ever memories I did not have, I would not regain back. I explained to him that when someone tells me something I kind of remember the story they are telling me, but I can never remember anything more about it; just what they tell me. He explained to me that I am not actually remembering being there or doing what they are explaining, that my mind wants to remember so it grabs it as a memory and defies me and makes me think that I remember it.

For years I fought what he said. I tried to act like they were my memories. But in my heart I knew that they were not. From that time on I could never come up with a memory of my own.

When doctor finally felt it would be safe for me to start taking the medications, he prescribed me a low dosage hoping that it might help. After taking just a few pills blood clots developed in my leg once again. I did not have to go into the hospital this time because the clots were small. I was given syringes and the medicine and was instructed to give myself two shots a day in the stomach.

It was horrible stabbing a needle in stomach and sometimes my body would refuse to allow me to put the pain upon my self and my hand would flinch causing me to have to puncture myself again. My stomach bruised so badly that it hurt to wear anything. But I had no choice, I had to torture myself.

Every year for seven years, I got blood clots in my leg again. The medicine to help the petit-mal seizures was no longer an option.

Sometimes I think how strange it is that it was the exact amount of time that the doctor said that if I did not get my memories back by then they would never return that the blood blots never formed again. Sometimes I wonder if someone in Heaven wanted it that way.

Chapter 9

For years to come everything would remain the same. I felt lost and uncertain to whom I was. People around me continued to talk of a person that I did not know, but that person was me.

Some believed me when I tell them that I do not understand who they are talking about, others thought I was making it up. This angered me. Why couldn't they accept who I was now and why would some think I was lying. I could not understand why they would think that someone would want to lie about such a horrific thing.

Some memories had returned, all of which are horrible and haunting. I would say that they were made up, but I talked to my husband about them and he agrees with me that they are true. I had told him about my dad before we were married and I had told him about my cousins and the other men also.

I was thirty something years old. Still confused about my life and left with only memories of torture and hate. But yet I had a husband who continued to stand by my side knowing that I didn't remember much about him; I don't even remember our wedding day. And I have three kids that loved me unconditionally and a Mother who continued to try and help me by telling me wonderful stories about my childhood. I always liked when she would do that, it helped me see that all my life was not always that of pain that there were times that I was happy.

But I had a secret that no one knew about. I was sad. I was so sad that I cried every night. I wanted to be the person that my family knew but I couldn't. I wanted to be the person that my husband fell in love with, but I couldn't. I felt because of this that at any moment my husband would walk out on me.

The death of the person that was lost (me) made me restless. I began moving my family from place to place trying to find out who I was. But no matter how much I moved us around, nothing worked. I could not find the person I was searching for. I was still lost.

I moved to Oklahoma and dragged my family along with me. I had family out there. I had seen their pictures and in the pictures everyone was smiling. I felt like maybe that is where I belonged. I lived down here for a short while when I was fourteen so I felt that if I went back down there it would spark something inside me and everything will be good again. My family in California was not able to help, maybe this place, these people would be the answer.

In Oklahoma I became a person I did not like. I was lost more then ever. I became more confused then ever. Men liked me here and constantly were paying attention to me. I liked the attention I was getting but at the same time I feared the men. I became more distant from my children and my husband.

I began to crave the attention I was getting. These people did not know my past so therefore they did not care. They liked me for who I was, and that was something that I felt like I had been missing for years.

I would go out dancing every weekend. It made me feel good, the people around me made me feel good about myself. I was happy but at the same time I was miserable.

My husband was working at Print shop in town; I was working at a store in the mall. I sold men's shoes. I liked it. I had not worked in years and I felt good about myself. That was until one day. My fear of men was confirmed that day. To this day I have not told my husband about what had happened. I think it is because I thought he would be mad at me and leave me. I did not want to be alone so I have kept my secret until now.

The man was a security guard for the store I worked in. I was in the back storage room getting some shoes for a customer that was waiting. I did not hear him come up behind me. But when I turned around he was there. I tried to get past him, but he was a big man, a muscular man, and he would not allow me to walk around him. I insisted that he let me by or I would scream. He placed his hand over my mouth and with the other hand grabbed inside my shirt. I was petrified. This man could kill me if he wanted.

I stood still, with only tears falling down my face. It seemed like he was there for ever, but I know it was only a matter of seconds. He suddenly turned around and walked out, never saying a word. I felt like I was in a nightmare. For some reason that day, I did not care. It had happened to me so many times that I was numb inside. I went on with my business, finished my day at work, but never returned to that store again.

Things got worst. Whenever I went out to see my favorite band my husband would go along. But it didn't matter, men ignored the fact that I was with someone and continuously tried to pick up on me. I ignored them and my husband would just laugh.

Then one night, we had been out dancing and were on our way home. I had asked my husband to stop at the store to get me a soda. He went in while I waited in the car. A group of men pulled up in a car beside us and began talking to me. I explained to them that I was married and that I was not interested. Then men waited for my husband to come out of the store and get in the car. As soon as he buckled the seatbelt the men attacked him through the window. I could not believe what was happening. By the time I had got inside to tell the cashier to call the police the fight was over and the men had left.

My husband was livid, but not at me, but at the men that had attacked him. He asked me what happened and I explained it to him. The whole situation made no sense at all. That is when I decided I could never tell him of the situation in the store. Deep inside I truthfully thought that all of this was my fault. What every it was that was warranting the reactions that men had toward me, was affecting my husband.

In fear that things would get worst, I quickly figured out that Oklahoma was not the place for me or my family.

I packed up our stuff and moved my family again.

Chapter 10

We moved back to California and bought a house. Now every since the day I died I had been having strange things happen. Things like seeing a black shadow or such things like someone touching me and no one be around, just weird things like that. But it wasn't until we moved into this house that things got worst. The house we bought we lived in for three months, then left.

For the first few days we lived there we loved the house. Then slowly things began to happen.

I loved angels and had been collecting them. I had shelves that I would set them on throughout the house. My husband and I seemed a little distant from one another then and every time he would walk by one of the shelves the angels would fall off and break. At first I thought he was bumping into them and that was why they were falling. But then one time he was in the bathroom and the shelf behind him flew off of the wall at him and hit him on the back, all of the Angels falling to the ground and breaking. The shelf was attached to the wall with six inch screws; there was no way a simple thing like someone bumping into it would cause the entire shelf to fall.

That was the beginning of the nightmares that house would bring.

There was a window seat that you could sit at and look out at the front yard. It was painted in white, but we noticed that red began seeping up through the paint. I would paint over the red but the next morning the unexplained red coloring would return. I tried painting the seat many times, but after every attempt failed, I covered it with cloth.

My sons, now 16 years old and 11 years old began experiencing things that were unexplainable. One night my son Jeffery and his friend were in his room. They said it sounded like a helicopter was landing in their room, and then it became cold. Suddenly a women manifested in the corner.

That was not the only experience that they had.

His friend had stayed the night one night. I was sleeping in the living room because something about my room frightened me. My husband worked nights so I always slept on the couch.

One night when I was sleeping I looked up and saw that my son's friend was standing at the stairs looking at me. He had a blank look on his face. It was like his body was there but his mind was elsewhere. I began screaming at him asking him what was he doing. He did not move. He could not hear me; he just continued to stare. I became very scared. I did not like the look on his face; it was almost sinister like.

Finally after screaming at him numerous times I was able to get his attention. After asking him what he was doing he explained to me that he had no idea why he was standing, nor how he got there. I made him go back to bed. The rest of that night I found it hard to sleep.

Things continued to worsen. No one felt comfortable being in the house and no one wanted to sleep in their rooms.

My niece moved in with us. It was her turn to become victim of the unknown haunting. One night my niece was taking a shower. Everyone was downstairs sitting at the kitchen table. My niece began to scream from the upstairs bathroom telling whomever it was that was knocking that she would be out soon. There was no one up there. When she came out of the shower she yelled down stairs asking why Cheyenne was bothering her while she was in the shower. We explained to her that no one up there while she was taking a shower. To this day she still insists that she heard Cheyenne talking to her and that she saw shadows under the door that night.

My husband and I began to fight for no

reason. We had never really argued before but it became an every night occurrence. It got to the point that you could feel the hatred that the house was omitting out.

We did not sell the house; we did not rent the house out. We packed our stuff up in one day and moved into another house that we owned.

The house that we moved to was a house that we owned that we were renting out. It was a home that we had left when we moved to Oklahoma. It was the only home that we knew that felt like our home. In fact it was the only house we lived in that ever did. I was happy to be home.

Before we had moved to Oklahoma we had redid the entire home with wallpaper and decorative paint. It was beautiful. The people that had lived there had taken it all down; it was now ugly and dingy.

As soon as we moved the tension that my husband and I were feeling toward one another ceased. And although I still suffered from the memory loss and the little seizures I was having, I was getting better. I loved my husband more and more everyday. He had never lost his love for me but for a while I was uncertain about mine to his. But now he and my children were my life.

Whatever it was that had haunted us in the other house followed us here. The same things began happening, but this time the entity was not evil, just mischievous. My husband always said it was me that was bringing the spirits. He says when I died I opened up something so that the spirits could follow me. I always laughed at him.

But with what happens later in my life I begin to agree with him.

The strangest of the unexplained things that was happening was that every time I would get upset the cold water in our bedroom will come on. There is no explanation to why this is happening. There were two sinks in our room. It was never the same faucet, but it was always the cold water.

After months of this happening we had a plumber come in to check the sinks. They could not find anything wrong.

The behavior of whatever was doing this was aiming its anger toward my husband.

One day as we were in the bedroom John was standing in front of my closet. He was upset with me for something; but I don't remember what it was. As he continued to talk to me in an angered tone my closet door opened and the stuff that was on the top shelf flew out at him. Was I somehow doing this? I don't see how.

This became a normal thing in the house and after a while we began to ignore it.

Finally things began to fit with me. I was happy and so was my family. I had started nursing school and was excited to help others. I did not what happened to me to happen to another person, and if I could just help one woman, then that would be one less person that would have to suffer as I had.

Going back to school was great for me. At first I was having problems.

There was a lot I did not know how to do; like basic math. But after a while I understood it and started doing much better.

I had become great friends with my mom. We talked everyday on the phone and I would go see her at least twice a month. She lived with my eldest sister and so it was only an hour drive from our house.

John and I had made plans to renew our vows. I never regained the memory of our wedding so we decided that we would take a cruise *(something we had wanted to do)* and renew our vows on the ship.

Things were going to good. I had madly fallen back in love with my husband and could not wait to marry him again. I had purchased a beautiful wedding gown of my dreams and fit perfectly.

That year John's brother died in a horrible train wreck. He was driving his motorcycle along a railroad track. He lost control and feel in front of a moving train. He was killed instantly.

My husband was devastated. I had known his brother since I was fourteen, but really had no memory of him. I felt bad for my husband and the pain he was feeling, but I fear I did not offer him the sympathy he needed; although I tried.

Chapter 11

It is March of 2002 only five months after my brother-in-law's death.

My in laws were still healing after their loss. Family get together were tough, but we would be having Easter at their house.

Because of my brother-in-law's death I felt that I needed to get some things settled. If I was to die, I wanted to die in peace and not be holding onto the sadness that continued to taunt me. I finally got up the courage to talk to my mom about the memories of my dad and other men that had hurt me, including a man that was a friend of my eldest sister.

I could have picked anyone to talk about this with but I picked her because I had to know if all these years she had known what had happened to me.

You could hear it in her voice that my words had devastated her. She swore to me that she had no idea about any of it and if she did she would taken care of it. She swore to me that she would never have allowed people to hurt me the way they did. I believed her.

A few days later we were to go to her house to visit. I was excited. I had not seen her in a few weeks and I loved to visit her. It was rainy out that day. The wind and rain would stop us from our visit. The wet freeway was dangerous and taking our children on such a drive was not an option. My husband and I decided that we would spend the day working on the house. A few hours into our work my husband decided he needed to get some more material from the store. We stop everything we were doing and drove up to the local hardware store. It was 11am so the store was not crowded.

As soon as we walk in the store a pain shoot through my heart. I felt as if I was having a heart attack. Then just as quickly as the pain came it disappeared.

After gathering our purchases we headed back home and continued working on adding crown molding to our walls. I did not worry about the pain I had felt again.

The phone rang. I don't know if it was the sound of the phone ringing mixing with the sound of the saw in the background that made me cringe, but the tone of the phone was eerie and like no other I have ever heard. I ignored the loud sound of the wood saw behind me and picked up the receiver. The constant buzzing of the wood being sawed in half restricted me from hearing the person on the other end of the phone.

I had to motion to my husband to shut off the tool that he was using so that I may hear the person better.
He was interested to whom I was talking to so he walked over and stood beside me.

It is my sister on the other end. She is trying to tell me something, but her words are muffled by her constant sobbing. My heart plummet's into my stomach.

There is something horribly wrong. I asked her again what it was that had her in such frenzy.

Her response is something that I was not prepared to hear.

I couldn't catch my breath, I couldn't breathe. My face became pale and my ears began to ring. I was going to pass out. With an expression of despair on my face, I looked over at my husband. Instantly, uncontrollable tears streamed down my cheeks. My Mother had passed away. I would never hear her voice again, nor see her beautiful smile. In my mind I was a young child who had lost her best friend, her mentor, her Mother. My knees had become weak. I could no longer stand up. I needed to sit down, but I confused, my mind was a boggle. I did not know what to do. I sat on the edge of the couch, buried my face in my hands and cried.

I had known my Mother for seven years out of my thirty years of life and now she was gone. I would never get the chance to know her as her other children did.

My oldest son was not home when I got

the call, so I had to call him so that he could come home. I wanted to get to my sisters as soon as possible. I could not accept the fact that my mother had passed away, so I had to see for myself.

When we arrived my sister was sitting outside her house with her two children. My other sister and I arrived at the same time so we walked up together. My oldest sister Lois refused to let us go in. She explained that the coroner had not gotten there yet and that our Mother was still lying on the floor. I did not care what she said; I was going to see my mom one last time. I told her that I had to use the bathroom. I walked past her and so that I did not lie to her I went into the bathroom. After only a second of being in there I walked into the living room. My mother was lying on the floor covered by a crotched blanket she had made. Kawnie the sister that is a year older then me was already sitting down next to her lifeless body. I sat down beside her and touched my mom. It was not my mom, she was cold and stiff not like the mother I knew. I wanted her to get up and laugh her funny little laugh. But she never moved. I was blank. I had no emotions to express. I just sat there with my hand resting on hers. My sister was crying, but my tears were lost somewhere within me.

A while later the coroner showed up. They insisted that her jewelry be removed before they took her away. No one would do it, so it was up to me. I stood over her while the man took her jewelry off and handed it to me. Everything that was happening did not feel real to me, so although it bothered me to some extent it did not seem to bother me as much as the others.

One of her rings became stuck on her finger. The man continued to pull on it. I knew she could not feel what was happening but it was bothering me. I was afraid that he was hurting her. I wanted him to stop!

After an hour the men were done. I had one last chance to say goodbye. I kissed her forehead as they were walking out.

Everyone was sitting in the living

room. But I did not want to be with any one of them. I snuck out to the front porch and sat in a chair. Within seconds I was crying with such intensity that I could no longer catch my breath. My heart had been ripped from my chest and stomped on. My sobbing quickly became out of control.

My nephew heard me from within the kitchen and came to sit with me, but there was no consoling me.

He held onto me as tight as he could. But I could not feel anything. I was numb to any other emotion beside the one I was feeling at that moment; complete and utter sadness.

After a while the entire family came out including my husband. I wanted to leave. I wanted to go home. I could not stand being there anymore. My mom was supposed to be there, but she was gone and would never be there again. It did not feel right to me to be in that house and not hear her laughter.

I explained to the rest of my family that I could not stay; I had to leave.

My husband agreed with me that it would be best. My sisters wanted me to stay but there was no way I could. I felt bad that I had to leave them, but I was no good to anyone in the state I was in. After saying goodbye we got in the car.

I was looking out at the others when something caught my eye. On the windshield in front of me were the words "I love you". The message had been written from inside the car and was not there when we had first arrived.

I began screaming at everyone in the car. I wanted to know who would do such a thing. My heart was broken and to me it was a horrible trick. Everyone denied doing it and my husband explained that the car had been locked since we arrived and that no one had been in there.

My mother would be cremated within three days; her funeral would be in four.

On the night she was being cremated I was sleeping in my bed. I was scared awake when a woman screamed in my ear *"Oh my god it hurts so bad, make it stop."* It was the voice of my dear departed mother. The cremation had hurt her, or so I felt. Instantly I became hysterical.

My husband was at work and my oldest son was out. My twelve year old son was the only one I had to speak to. I ran into his room. Tears were streaming down my face and I could barley talk. I sat on his bed as he held my hand in his and tried to help me forget what had happened.

There is no fixing a broken heart until it is ready to mend itself. It is my 34th birthday, the day my mother would be buried. I felt as I did seven years ago, lost and uncertain to whom I am. At any moment the house would fill with family and friends, all of which want to say their final goodbyes to my Mother.

My sisters and I are running some errands before everyone gets there. My mother had put a ring on layaway for me, so we were headed to the pawn shop to get it out. My eldest sister Lois wanted to give it to her son so that he could give it to his Fiancé. This broke my heart. She could have cared less that the ring was meant for me.

After talking to her son I finally got him to call her and tell her that he did not the ring; that was meant for me and so that is who should get it.

My mother had life insurance, but that money would not be used to retrieve it. I was told by my oldest sister that I wanted the ring I would have to pay for it myself. I took my husbands paycheck and that is the money I used.

I had no idea what the ring looked like. All I knew was that it was wedding ring that she had picked out for me.

My husband and I had lost my ring when I was sick; we could no longer make the payments.

The ring was beautiful. It was exactly what I would have picked out for myself.

By the time we got back to my sisters house, people had already started arriving. I tried to talk to everyone that came up to me. Some I knew, but most I didn't. They were still lost in my memories; that I felt would never be found. It was all too much for me to handle. I wanted my Mom!

I ran into her room and held her pillow as tight as I could against my chest. The strangers that had come to honor my mother walked by, staring into the room, looking at me with their expressions of concern. No one said a word, but through their expressions in their eyes you could see that were hurting also.

I rested my weary body on her bed, crying into her pillow, crying with the need for someone to take the pain away. I felt that there was no one that could do that. I was a stranger to most that were there as they were too me.

I closed my eyes and let the smell of her perfume overtake my sense of need. My brother walked in. I had known him as a child, but since my sickness I did not know him anymore. He sat next to me on the bed, placed his hand on my head and runs his fingers through my hair.

He conveyed to me that our Mom would never have wanted to see me like this. He said that he understood that I probably was having a harder time dealing with the loss then anyone else.

Not only was I the youngest of the children, but because of my memory loss he understood that I must have been in a lot of pain. He offered his sympathy to me. But I knew he really did not know me, so in my heart it meant very little.

The last time I had seen him was when I was a child. He didn't know me like he tried to insist that he did. He was just trying to be nice. At least at that moment that is how I felt.

I had never asked anyone for help. I guess I thought they really didn't care. But he did, and come to find out so did many others.

It is funny how such a tragedy can help you see that for years you have been blinded to the people around you that have wanted to help you. My memories had not faded with my mom's passing; it opened a door so that others could share new ones with me.

Chapter 12

No one would have thought that my mother's death would have affected me as it did. I become so depressed that the only thing that I could do was cry. I no longer wanted to talk to anyone, nor see anyone. I lost 40 pounds in two months. My body was fading away and so was my heart.

My depression became so bad that my husband talked to some of his friends and family and asked if they would please call me and talk to me. Nothing helped. I don't think I really ever listened to what they had to say.

In my heart and in my mind I was young child, someone who had just met their mother and now she was gone.

I had finished my semester in

school, but barley passed. After my mom had passed away my grades had began to fail. I could not concentrate and studying was just about impossible. I wanted to make her proud, but my depression was winning.

I let the depression overtake me to the point where I would not leave the house. And then I became afraid to leave the house. Things got worst and I became afraid to be alone.

My mother had died while she was alone and now I feared that I would suffer the same fate if I were ever left by myself.

The time had come, I had gone through all the classes I needed; four years in college to be exact, and now I ready for my nursing degree. I had received my acceptance letter in the mail. But I was not excited as I should have been. I no longer cared about school. I no longer cared what happened to others. I was sad and nothing mattered anymore.

My husband became more worried then ever. I refused to go

anywhere to see anyone. I sat in my room and only held my mothers pillow in my arms.

School for the children was coming soon and that meant I would be alone once again. I could feel the panic grow inside of me as the time came closer. I was deathly afraid of being alone.

I came up with a plan. We would sell our home and take the money and move to Iowa and start business. That way I would never have to be alone again. Besides I had family out there and I felt that besides my Family in the high desert they were the only family that cared about me anymore.

My eldest sister, the one who my mother lived with, never really liked me. And I had found out from her that she believed that my memory loss was fabricated by me so that I could attention from my family. After that we never really talked again.

We sold the house, packed all our things and moved to Iowa. We started our own business, and I was doing better.

WHAT DID YOU SAY MY NAME WAS?

I really enjoyed seeing my family and they had many more memories to share with me.

Our business was taking off and doing pretty good. We had been in Iowa for about two months when I got phone call from my sister. She informed me that our eldest sister had been found in the shower. She had died. I felt sad, but not like the sadness I felt with my Mother's death. I was more angry then anything. This woman never liked me and never gave me a chance, but always loved everyone else. Now she would never get the chance to know me, nor would I get the chance to know her.

We had put all our money in our business, so there was none for me to use to go to her funeral. I would have to fly there and with our money all used up that was not an option.

Her daughter became angry with me that I did not come to her mom's funeral and vowed to never talk to me again. She has stuck to that and I never hear from her. My sister still receives phone calls quite often from my niece and nephew, but to them it is like I am no longer alive.

Already use to heartbreak, I continued on with my life.

A few months passed and I asked my closest sister to come visit me. I had not seen her in a year and I felt like I had lost so many people in my life I needed to see her before anything bad happened to her or me.

It was the day she was to leave. I got a phone call from her step daughter informing me that she was in the hospital, but she was trying to still make it to the plane. I thought they were lying. That maybe my sister had decided that she did not want to come down, so she was making the story up.

I called the hospital and found out that her story was true. She was suffering from pneumatic fever. She was very ill. She would not be making the plane.

For days I called every hour on the hour to find out how she was doing. I was told that if I could I should get down to California and see her, they were not sure if she was going to make it very much longer. I was heartbroken.

That same week, I was visited by my Uncle. He had also been in the hospital and was released that day. He stopped by our shop to talk to me. His words were heart wrenching. He explained to me that they found out that he had stomach cancer. He said that they gave him two months to live. He had decided not to go through Chemotherapy because he was already suffering from emphysema.

I knew right away that it would only be maybe a week or two before he would die.

Now I had a sister dying in California and an Uncle dying in Iowa. I was a mess. Every time I let someone into my heart, they would pass away. I did not know if I was coming or going.

I did not know if I should stay in Iowa or go see my sister in California. I called the hospital again. My sister's husband said that she was going to be fine and that I did not need to go down there. Uncertain if I could believe him I called back and talked to a nurse. I was told by the nurse that I should get down there as soon as possible. I was confused to say the least.

Later on that day relief came when my sister called and said that she was doing better and that I should stay and be with our uncle.

Everyone from my Uncles side came down to be with him. We closed our business for the week so that we could be with him as much as possible. All day the family would get together over at my Aunts house. It seemed like it was only a day or two before he became unaware of anyone's presence. The pain pills had taken over and although he was their in body he was longer there in mind.

We had few good days with him before he was lost. He died two weeks later; but he died with his family around him.

Chapter 13

Our business stalled and then plummeted into nothingness after my Uncles death. We had some customers that did not pay their bills which in turn made it where we lost everything.

We moved back to California so that my husband could get a job. My sister was out of the hospital and said that we could stay with her for a while until we can find a place to live.

We left everything we owned in Iowa, packed some clothing and took our kids and animals with us.

We had only enough money for gas and a little bit of food. We had left in the winter time so it was cold. We would have to sleep in the car because there just was not enough money to get a hotel room and there were not enough drivers to drive straight through.

The one night that we stopped to sleep it was -10 degrees out. The car became so cold that no one could sleep. We were freezing. While my husband continued to try and get some rest I would turn on the car, warm it up, then turn it back off in fear that we would use up to much gas. Never the less we only got about three hours rest that night.

When we got to my sisters I knew that she was still sick. The first time I saw her I wanted to cry. Her hair had fallen out and she looked like death. I kept my feelings in and never showed her the sorrow I was experiencing.

She lived in a small singlewide mobile home so my two kids had to sleep on the couch. My oldest son had moved in with a friend so he was no longer living with us. My husband and I stayed in a small room just big enough for a single bed. There was no place for our clothing so we kept them in plastic garbage bags.

The situation was bad. We were thankful for the place to live but we were miserable at the same time.

My husband and I began to fight almost constantly. For the first time I was being blamed for everything that was happening with our lives. In my heart I knew he was right. If I had not died that night none of what I had done to my family would have happened.

But now a new disease had began to plague me. I had contracted a disease that caused me to be constantly dizzy. I could no longer drive, nor work because of it. Once again I could not offer any help. It would be a while before we could afford a home of our own. The weight of our family would have to rest on my husband. It was not fair, but there was nothing I could do to help.

Because there was no room at my sisters and my husband was so miserable we decided to move in with my husband's sister. They lived in a larger home but they did not have an extra bedroom for us to sleep in. The four of us slept in the living room.

This did not last long. Their kids and our kids began to fight with one another and it became obvious that we needed to leave before our families began to hate one another.

We saved our money and rented a small house in Palmdale. The house was old and dirty but we tried to make it our home.

My daughter quickly became friends with some sweet little girls next door. It was summer time so school was out for vacation. The three little girls would play in the front yard in a blow up pool. It was always hot outside so it was their only way of cooling off. The girls were all about nine years old. Innocent children, and did not notice at first the man across the street that had been watching them.

One day after we pulled into our driveway we saw a light flash, then another. We looked across the street and saw a man hiding in the bushes; he had been taking pictures of the young girls.

My husband was livid. Without hesitation he ran across the street, grabbed the camera from the man and through the camera to the ground. The man had been taking pictures of these three little girls for weeks.

That night I looked him up on the registered offender list. He was there. I would not allow my daughter become a victim like me. We moved that weekend.

For a year we moved from one house to another. It wasn't that we wanted to move but the houses we would move into would be in foreclosure and the owners would forget to tell us that. There for a while it seemed like every three months we were looking for a new home to move to.

I was getting tired of packing and soon refused to totally unpack anymore.

I found a singlewide mobile home that someone was selling and decided that would be the best way to go. My husband was working and it would be easy to make the payments.

Although the house only had two bedrooms; we moved in. The two children had to share a room. This was hard as my son was sixteen and my daughter was eleven; neither one of them would ever get any privacy.

The mobile home was never a home, just a place for us to stay.

It took us three years to pay the mobile home off. Finally we would have some breathing room.

We saved our money and decided to venture into the café business. We knew someone who was leasing out a bar with a café. We sunk every penny into the business plus more. The first week it looked like the business was going to boom. We were busy all the time, so busy in fact that I was working seven days a week, sixteen hours a day. My sister had started working with us to help us out. It looked like for once something good was going to happen to us.

One Saturday morning we got up. We had to open the restaurant so my sister, my husband and I drove together, As soon as we pulled up, my sister-n-law pulled into the driveway. She was crying. Her husband got out of the car and walked up to my husband. My father-n-law had died. In a matter of a year and a half we had now lost five close family members.

We left the restaurant to my sister to tend to that day and went to my mother-n-laws. By the time we got there most of the family was already there. It was a sad day. I had known Jack since I fourteen years old. Not only was he my father-n-law he was my friend.

I always considered him my dad because my dad had died when I was twenty two years old and the memories I was left with were the ones of how he hurt me so. So to me, Jack was the only Father I ever knew.

My heart was broken and so my husbands. For a week we did not return to the bar. My sister and some of her family ran it for us. Things were slow there, so by the time I returned to work there was no money to keep the bar open. I closed the doors the next day; I could no longer fund the place.

My sister became angry at me and accused me of holding back money. For months she refused to talk to me.

Once again things began to get

bad. My husband's work began to slow. We had been having a hard time paying our bills, but with the home now being paid for we would finally have a little extra money for food.

Within a month my husband's job cut his hours to less then half time. We no longer could pay for anything; not even the space rent. We were starving and on the brink of loosing the only place we had to live. We had no other choice, we had to sell the home for dirt cheap so that we could pay the park what we owed them and have enough money to move into a rental.

We sold the house for 4500 dollars. It gave us just enough to rent a home and move. At first it seemed like my husbands work was going to pick up and we would do better. But then the economy took a dive. Once gain we were starving. Our food diminished and we were left with only bologna sandwiches to eat for breakfast, lunch and dinner.

Because rents are cheaper in Iowa and my husband was offered a job out there, we moved again.

We put all our stuff in storage put two kids, five cats, seven kittens and one small dog in our car and left. We could make it here, but it would be tight.

We had found a small mobile home and bought it for two thousand dollars.

It is not a home, only a place we stay. I do hope that some day we will find a home again and that I can settle down and enjoy whatever years I have left.

I continue to suffer from dizziness, but I am learning to live with it. Sometimes it is bad, others it is minimal, but it is always there. I have finally found out who I am. I am a Mother, a wife, a sister and friend to people who really care for me. That is all that matters. The past is the past, and although I still think back to the horrible memories that remain, I know now it is time to look forward to my future.

People do stupid things in their lives; it is up to you to choose to forgive them.

SHAWNA LYNN STEWART

"My memories remain hostage within me, but the love I have to offer my family and friends is finally free"

Be sure to check out other

Books Written By *Shawna Lynn Stewart*

Lessons from an Evil Mind > Seeded From Evil
By *Shawna Lynn*

Children Books by *Shawna Stewart*
The Barnyard Boogie

Mary and the Magical Magnifying Glass

SHAWNA LYNN STEWART

Lightning Source UK Ltd.
Milton Keynes UK
UKOW051216051211

183232UK00001B/63/P